Blank Cookbook : Recipes & Notes

Recipe Index

Recipe Name	Page

Notes

Recipe Index

Recipe Name	Page

Notes

Recipe Index

Recipe Name	Page

Notes

Recipe Index

Recipe Name	Page

Notes

_____

Recipe

Serves _____ Prep Time _____ Cook Time _____ Oven Temp _____

Ingredients	Directions

Notes

Recipe

Serves_____ Prep Time_____ Cook Time_____ Oven Temp_____

Ingredients

Directions

Notes

Recipe

Serves _____ Prep Time _____ Cook Time _____ Oven Temp _____

Ingredients

Directions

Notes

Recipe

_____

Serves ____ Prep Time _____ Cook Time _____ Oven Temp ____

Ingredients	Directions

Notes

Recipe

Serves_____ Prep Time_____ Cook Time_____ Oven Temp_____

Ingredients

Directions

Notes

_____

Recipe

Serves ____ Prep Time _____ Cook Time _____ Oven Temp ____

Ingredients

Directions

Notes

Page ____

_____

Recipe

Serves _____ Prep Time _____ Cook Time _____ Oven Temp _____

Ingredients | ## Directions

_____ | _____
_____ | _____
_____ | _____
_____ | _____
_____ | _____
_____ | _____
_____ | _____
_____ | _____
_____ | _____
_____ | _____
_____ | _____
_____ | _____
_____ | _____
_____ | _____
_____ | _____
_____ | _____
_____ | _____

Notes

Recipe

Serves _____ Prep Time _____ Cook Time _____ Oven Temp _____

Ingredients

Directions

Notes

Recipe

Serves ___ Prep Time ___ Cook Time ___ Oven Temp ___

Ingredients

Directions

Notes

Recipe

Serves_____ Prep Time_____ Cook Time_____ Oven Temp_____

Ingredients

Directions

Notes

Recipe

Serves_____ Prep Time_____ Cook Time_____ Oven Temp_____

Ingredients

Directions

Notes

Page _____

_____

Recipe

Serves _____ Prep Time _____ Cook Time _____ Oven Temp _____

Ingredients

Directions

Notes

Recipe

Serves____ Prep Time____ Cook Time____ Oven Temp____

Ingredients

Directions

Notes

_____

Recipe

Serves ___ Prep Time _____ Cook Time _____ Oven Temp ___

Ingredients

Directions

Notes

Recipe

Serves _____ Prep Time _____ Cook Time _____ Oven Temp _____

Ingredients

Directions

Notes

Recipe

Serves ___ Prep Time ___ Cook Time ___ Oven Temp ___

Ingredients

Directions

Notes

Recipe

Serves_____ Prep Time_____ Cook Time_____ Oven Temp_____

Ingredients

Directions

Notes

_____

Recipe

Serves _____ Prep Time _____ Cook Time _____ Oven Temp _____

Ingredients

Directions

Notes

Recipe

Serves ____ Prep Time _____ Cook Time _____ Oven Temp ____

Ingredients

Directions

Notes

Recipe

Serves _____ Prep Time _____ Cook Time _____ Oven Temp _____

Ingredients

Directions

Notes

_____

Recipe

Serves ____ Prep Time _____ Cook Time _____ Oven Temp ____

Ingredients

Directions

Notes

_____

Recipe

Serves _____ Prep Time _____ Cook Time _____ Oven Temp _____

Ingredients

Directions

Notes

Page _____

Recipe

Serves ____ Prep Time ____ Cook Time ____ Oven Temp ____

Ingredients

Directions

Notes

_____

Recipe

Serves _____ Prep Time _____ Cook Time _____ Oven Temp _____

Ingredients

Directions

Notes

Recipe

Serves____ Prep Time____ Cook Time____ Oven Temp____

Ingredients

Directions

Notes

_____

Recipe

Serves ___ Prep Time_____ Cook Time_____ Oven Temp___

Ingredients

Directions

Notes

Page _____

Recipe

Serves _____ Prep Time _____ Cook Time _____ Oven Temp _____

Ingredients

Directions

Notes

Recipe

_____

Serves _____ Prep Time _____ Cook Time _____ Oven Temp _____

Ingredients

Directions

Notes

Recipe

Serves____ Prep Time_____ Cook Time_____ Oven Temp____

Ingredients

Directions

Notes

Recipe

Serves ___ Prep Time ___ Cook Time ___ Oven Temp ___

Ingredients

Directions

Notes

Page ___

Recipe

Serves_____ Prep Time_____ Cook Time_____ Oven Temp_____

Ingredients

Directions

Notes

_____

Recipe

Serves____ Prep Time_____ Cook Time_____ Oven Temp____

Ingredients

Directions

Notes

Recipe

Serves _____ Prep Time _____ Cook Time _____ Oven Temp _____

Ingredients

Directions

Notes

Recipe

Serves _____ Prep Time _____ Cook Time _____ Oven Temp _____

Ingredients

Directions

Notes

Recipe

Serves _____ Prep Time _____ Cook Time _____ Oven Temp _____

Ingredients

Directions

Notes

Recipe

Serves _____ Prep Time _____ Cook Time _____ Oven Temp _____

Ingredients

Directions

Notes

Recipe

Serves _____ Prep Time _____ Cook Time _____ Oven Temp _____

Ingredients

Directions

Notes

_____

Recipe

Serves____ Prep Time_____ Cook Time_____ Oven Temp____

Ingredients

Directions

Notes

_____

Recipe

Serves ____ Prep Time ____ Cook Time ____ Oven Temp ____

Ingredients

Directions

Notes

_____

Recipe

Serves _____ Prep Time _____ Cook Time _____ Oven Temp _____

Ingredients

Directions

Notes

Recipe

Serves _____ Prep Time _____ Cook Time _____ Oven Temp _____

Ingredients

Directions

Notes

Recipe

Serves _____ Prep Time _____ Cook Time _____ Oven Temp _____

Ingredients

Directions

Notes

_____

Recipe

Serves _____ Prep Time _____ Cook Time _____ Oven Temp _____

Ingredients

Directions

Notes

_____

Recipe

*Serves*____ *Prep Time*_____ *Cook Time*_____ *Oven Temp*____

Ingredients

Directions

Notes

Recipe

Serves ____ Prep Time _____ Cook Time _____ Oven Temp ____

Ingredients

Directions

Notes

Recipe

Serves____ Prep Time_____ Cook Time_____ Oven Temp____

Ingredients

Directions

Notes

_____

Recipe

Serves ____ Prep Time _____ Cook Time _____ Oven Temp ____

Ingredients   ## Directions

_____   _____
_____   _____
_____   _____
_____   _____
_____   _____
_____   _____
_____   _____
_____   _____
_____   _____
_____   _____
_____   _____
_____   _____
_____   _____
_____   _____
_____   _____
_____   _____
_____   _____
_____   _____

Notes

_____

Recipe

Serves ____ Prep Time _____ Cook Time _____ Oven Temp ____

Ingredients

Directions

Notes

Recipe

Serves _____ Prep Time _____ Cook Time _____ Oven Temp _____

Ingredients

Directions

Notes

_____

Recipe

Serves ____ Prep Time _____ Cook Time _____ Oven Temp _____

Ingredients

Directions

Notes

Page _____

_____

Recipe

Serves _____ Prep Time _____ Cook Time _____ Oven Temp _____

Ingredients

Directions

Notes

Recipe

Serves ___ Prep Time ___ Cook Time ___ Oven Temp ___

Ingredients

Directions

Notes

Recipe

Serves _____ Prep Time _____ Cook Time _____ Oven Temp _____

Ingredients

Directions

Notes

Recipe

Serves____ Prep Time____ Cook Time____ Oven Temp____

Ingredients

Directions

Notes

_____

Recipe

Serves ____ Prep Time _____ Cook Time _____ Oven Temp _____

Ingredients

Directions

Notes

Recipe

Serves ___ Prep Time ___ Cook Time ___ Oven Temp ___

Ingredients

Directions

Notes

Page ___

Recipe

Serves _____ Prep Time _____ Cook Time _____ Oven Temp _____

Ingredients

Directions

Notes

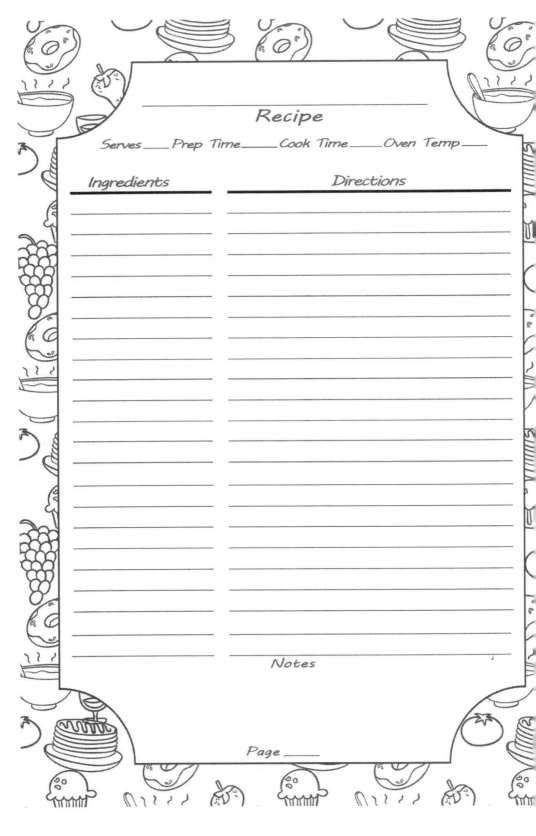

Recipe

_____

Serves ____ Prep Time ____ Cook Time ____ Oven Temp ____

Ingredients

Directions

Notes

Recipe

Serves ____ Prep Time ____ Cook Time ____ Oven Temp ____

Ingredients

Directions

Notes

_____

Recipe

*Serves*____ *Prep Time*_____ *Cook Time*_____ *Oven Temp*____

Ingredients	Directions

Notes

Recipe

Serves____ Prep Time_____ Cook Time_____ Oven Temp_____

Ingredients

Directions

Notes

Recipe

Serves ____ Prep Time ____ Cook Time ____ Oven Temp ____

Ingredients

Directions

Notes

Page ____

Recipe

Serves _____ Prep Time _____ Cook Time _____ Oven Temp _____

Ingredients

Directions

Notes

Recipe

Serves_____ Prep Time_____ Cook Time_____ Oven Temp_____

Ingredients

Directions

Notes

Recipe

Serves _____ Prep Time _____ Cook Time _____ Oven Temp _____

Ingredients

Directions

Notes

Recipe

Serves ____ Prep Time ____ Cook Time ____ Oven Temp ____

Ingredients

Directions

Notes

_____

Recipe

Serves _____ Prep Time _____ Cook Time _____ Oven Temp _____

Ingredients

Directions

Notes

Recipe

Serves____ Prep Time_____ Cook Time_____ Oven Temp____

Ingredients

Directions

Notes

Page____

Recipe

Serves_____ Prep Time_____ Cook Time_____ Oven Temp_____

Ingredients

Directions

Notes

_____

Recipe

Serves_____ Prep Time_____ Cook Time_____ Oven Temp____

Ingredients

Directions

_____
_____
_____
_____
_____
_____
_____
_____
_____
_____
_____
_____
_____
_____
_____
_____
_____
_____
_____
_____
_____

Notes

Recipe

Serves_____ Prep Time_____ Cook Time_____ Oven Temp_____

Ingredients

Directions

Notes

Recipe

Serves_____ Prep Time_____ Cook Time_____ Oven Temp_____

Ingredients

Directions

Notes

Page_____

Recipe

Serves _____ Prep Time _____ Cook Time _____ Oven Temp _____

Ingredients

Directions

Notes

Recipe

Serves____ Prep Time_____ Cook Time_____ Oven Temp____

Ingredients

Directions

Notes

Recipe

Serves_____ Prep Time_____ Cook Time_____ Oven Temp_____

Ingredients

Directions

Notes

_____

Recipe

Serves _____ Prep Time _____ Cook Time _____ Oven Temp _____

Ingredients	**Directions**

Notes

Recipe

Serves _____ Prep Time _____ Cook Time _____ Oven Temp _____

Ingredients

Directions

Notes

Recipe

Serves _____ Prep Time _____ Cook Time _____ Oven Temp _____

Ingredients

Directions

Notes

Recipe

Serves____ Prep Time_____ Cook Time_____ Oven Temp_____

Ingredients

Directions

Notes

Recipe

Serves _____ Prep Time _____ Cook Time _____ Oven Temp _____

Ingredients

Directions

Notes

Recipe

Serves _____ Prep Time _____ Cook Time _____ Oven Temp _____

Ingredients

Directions

Notes

Page _____

_____

Recipe

Serves____ Prep Time_____ Cook Time_____ Oven Temp____

Ingredients

Directions

Notes

Recipe

Serves ___ Prep Time ___ Cook Time ___ Oven Temp ___

Ingredients

Directions

Notes

Recipe

Serves _____ Prep Time _____ Cook Time _____ Oven Temp _____

Ingredients

Directions

Notes

Recipe

Serves _____ Prep Time _____ Cook Time _____ Oven Temp _____

Ingredients	Directions

Notes

Recipe

Serves _____ Prep Time _____ Cook Time _____ Oven Temp _____

Ingredients

Directions

Notes

Page _____

Recipe

Serves____ Prep Time_____ Cook Time_____ Oven Temp_____

Ingredients

Directions

Notes

_____

Recipe

Serves ____ Prep Time _____ Cook Time _____ Oven Temp _____

Ingredients

Directions

_____

_____

_____

_____

_____

_____

_____

_____

_____

_____

_____

_____

_____

_____

_____

_____

_____

_____

_____

_____

_____

_____

Notes

Page _____

Recipe

Serves _____ Prep Time _____ Cook Time _____ Oven Temp _____

Ingredients

Directions

Notes

Recipe

Serves ___ Prep Time ___ Cook Time ___ Oven Temp ___

Ingredients

Directions

Notes

Recipe

Serves_____ Prep Time_____ Cook Time_____ Oven Temp_____

Ingredients

Directions

Notes

_____

Recipe

Serves____ Prep Time____ Cook Time____ Oven Temp____

Ingredients

Directions

Notes

Recipe

Serves _____ Prep Time _____ Cook Time _____ Oven Temp _____

Ingredients

Directions

Notes

Recipe

Serves _____ Prep Time _____ Cook Time _____ Oven Temp _____

Ingredients

Directions

Notes

_____

Recipe

Serves _____ Prep Time _____ Cook Time _____ Oven Temp _____

Ingredients

Directions

Notes

Recipe

Serves ___ Prep Time ___ Cook Time ___ Oven Temp ___

Ingredients

Directions

Notes

Recipe

Serves _____ Prep Time _____ Cook Time _____ Oven Temp _____

Ingredients

Directions

Notes

_____

Recipe

Serves____ Prep Time_____ Cook Time_____ Oven Temp____

Ingredients

Directions

Notes

Page _____

Recipe

Serves _____ Prep Time _____ Cook Time _____ Oven Temp _____

Ingredients

Directions

Notes

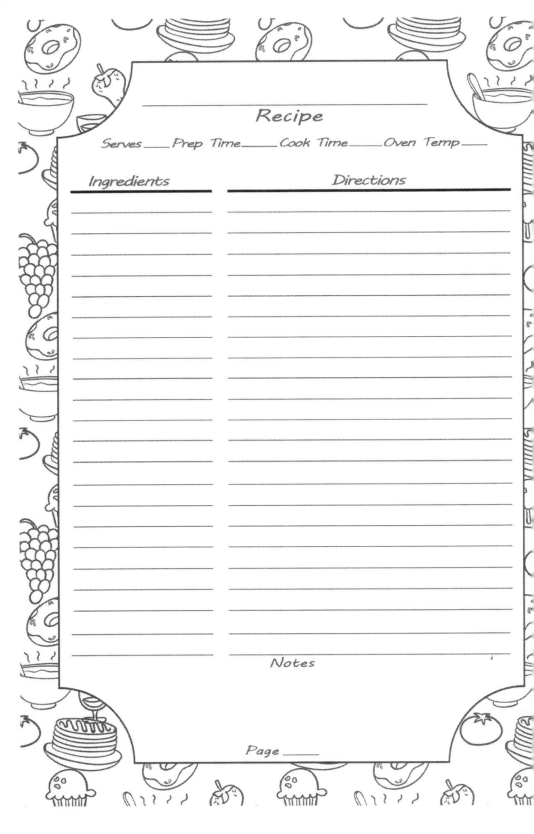

_____

Recipe

Serves ____ Prep Time _____ Cook Time _____ Oven Temp ____

Ingredients

Directions

Notes

Page ____

Recipe

Serves_____ Prep Time_____ Cook Time_____ Oven Temp_____

Ingredients

Directions

Notes

Need Another Blank Cookbook?
Visit www.blankbooksnjournals.com

63443956R00061

Made in the USA
Lexington, KY
07 May 2017